PLAYLIST

PITT POETRY SERIES ED OCHESTER, EDITOR

PLAYLIST

A POEM BY DAVID LEHMAN

UNIVERSITY OF PITTSBURGH PRESS

Published by the University of Pittsburgh Press, Pittsburgh, Pa., 15260
Copyright © 2019, David Lehman
Manufactured in the United States of America
Printed on acid-free paper
10 9 8 7 6 5 4 3 2 1

ISBN 10: 0-8229-6584-4
ISBN 13: 978-0-8229-6584-8

Cover art: Henri Matisse, *The Piano Lesson*, 1916, oil on canvas, 8' ½" × 6' 11¾"
(245.1 × 212.7 cm), Museum of Modern Art, New York.
Cover design: Joel W. Coggins

CONTENTS

A NOTE TO THE READER

Writing a poetry round-up for *Newsday* in 1975, I got to proclaim the greatness of A. R. Ammons's book-length poem *Sphere: The Form of a Motion* (1974). I wanted to meet the author. So when, a summer later, I began a four-year stint as an assistant professor at Hamilton College, it made sense to plan a day-trip from Clinton, New York, where Hamilton is located, to Ithaca, New York, home of Cornell University, where Ammons taught. A little over a hundred miles separates the two places, and some of it is on pleasant country roads.

Hospitable by nature, Archie greeted me in his office at Goldwin Smith Hall, showed me the headquarters of *Epoch* magazine, and took me for a walk around the arts quad and adjacent places on the Cornell campus. I recount the experience and part of our conversation in the entry of 11/29/17 of *Playlist*.

That visit began a deep and enduring friendship.

It was largely thanks to Archie that Cornell University's Society for the Humanities awarded me a postdoctoral fellowship for the year 1980–81. I have spent at least a part of every year since in Ithaca, so Archie and I got to be neighbors, then friends, then collaborators and coconspirators. Archie was a lively conversationalist, an excellent correspondent, and a most encouraging mentor. His wife Phyllis, who was as devoted to him as he was to her, was a legendary baker and enthusiastic host, and as her interest in the stock market matched mine, we always had plenty to talk about. I remember "the juice of three oranges" that she served on one fall day because the phrase made its way into an epistolary exchange that Archie and I had in 1989 and 1990. Archie played piano and at least twice there were spontaneous sing-alongs at their place. In 1992 I got to throw a Thanksgiving party, and Archie and Phyllis came and he read "Triphammer Bridge" aloud at my request.

Archie died in February 2001, a week.after he turned seventy-five. When I edited a volume of his selected poems for the Library of

America in 2006, it was the culmination of many years immersion in his work. Back in 1983 or 1984 I introduced readers of London's *Times Literary Supplement* to Ammons's poetry. Archie was the guest editor of the 1994 edition of *The Best American Poetry*, on which we worked together closely and happily. In 1996 I conducted his *Paris Review* interview. He and I also made several memorable joint appearances, and twice we conversed about his poems for the local public access TV station in Ithaca. The memories are joyous. The absence hurts. The ghost lingers.

Written on the daily installment plan from December 6, 1963, through January 10, 1964, Ammons's *Tape for the Turn of the Year* holds a special charm for me. Composed in the same fashion from November 20, 2017, through January 15, 2018, *Playlist* is dedicated to Archie, whose phone number I still know by heart, as the entry for 11/30 attests.

PLAYLIST

Dear Archie, today
I drove past 606 Hanshaw Road
where you haven't lived
since 1993, and where

you had green shutters
the currant occupants
have maroon ones. Yours
were better. You left us

in February 2001, a week before
you would have turned seventy-five.
I thought of your coil
of tape for the turn

of the year while I was driving
and listening to the radio
and deciding I would write
this poem to you, old friend,

now that I'm the age you were
when we edited a book together
and you were so much older then
than I. If you were here you

would ask me what about
the radio enchants me so much?
Its randomness, I would say.
Someone else is choosing

the order, the sequence
which may never cohere into sense,
but the day is like that,
it gives you what it has

and lets you arrange it
and sometimes you luck into
Sinatra singing "The Song Is You"
arranged by Billy May in 1958

and you understand that, Archie,
you remember the phone call
when I sang "it seems to me I've heard
that song before" and you sang

back "it's from an old familiar score"
you knew all the words
and reminded me that
you didn't have a radio in your Toyota (which

I can still see in your driveway) but
you didn't need a radio,
because you had
a very entertaining mind.

It's November 21
Tomorrow JFK will get assassinated
the late Hoagy Carmichael, born on the 22nd
in 1899, will play
"Among My Souvenirs"
in *The Best Years of our Lives*,
and Matthew Zapruder will turn fifty

But today,
today I take my Audi out for a spin
across various bridges
spanning the gorges of Ithaca
under a brilliant blue sky
darkening as I drive
and continuing to do so
after I step out of the car
and onto my favorite perch
above Cayuga's waters, the porch
where majestic trees devoid of leaves
stand like scarecrows
the sky a deeper hue an orange
and blue blaze dipping
below the horizon

The car radio is on
Sirius 71
and my mind wanders
I think how brilliant the bridges are
in "Isn't This a Lovely Day"
(Irving Berlin) and "Can't Help

Lovin' That Man of Mine" (Jerome
Kern, who also wrote the music for
"The Way You Look Tonight")

And that ("The Way You Look Tonight")
is playing
on the kitchen radio right now
with Coleman Hawkins on tenor sax
(whose birthday is today)
and tremendous sidemen
Max Roach, Milt Jackson, et al,
so WKCR is doing all Hawkins
all day as they have done since
the Johnson administration
(Lyndon, not Andrew)

And now I am nursing my Gibson
with gin from a Chicago distillery
having made a sidecar for Stacey
and had a quiet moment with Dean Martin
"Under the Bridges" and Keely Smith
can't think of anything I'd rather do

A good day for a drive to the country
underneath the apple tree with Carmen McRae
proving you can sing and talk at the same time
"and hear the bluebirds sing" she sings as if
there were a hyphen separating "blue" from "birds"
and we "shoot up" with summertime

Seventy-two hours have passed since
my momentous decision to organize
a poem around the symphonies
and songs I hear on the radio
on consecutive days as fall
fades into the early darkness of winter,
and I'm still up for
a jazz version of Stravinsky
while Harry "Sweets" Edison isn't misbehaving
I just spent a dizzy night in Tunisia
and word reaches me that Jennifer Lawrence
will play the lead in a soon-to-be-released
female-empowerment thriller
in which she is a Soviet agent or double agent
back in the day

"Lover" sings Peggy Lee as if it weren't a waltz
She's been there she knows it's time for black coffee
Is that Dean Martin yes it is
Dance with me make me sway
sway me more
I can't believe the song that
ends with "the meaning of existence O my love"
and then comes "Mack the Knife" as Louis Armstrong
does it first on the trumpet then with his sandpaper voice
when the shark bites and on the sidewalk, Sunday morning,
oozing life, the hero of the German intelligentsia is on stage
did our boy do something rash?
with the moon shining over Soho
"love will last, or it won't, here or some other place"

I'd be a beggar or a knave for you
Peggy Lee, "Why Don't You Do Right?"
and why Lee Wiley?
you'll find my reasoning is logically sound
and if that isn't love it'll have to do

Back in your own backyard
Jo Stafford's impeccable tail for "Embraceable You"
and Helen Forrest, who sang
"All the Things You Are" with Artie Shaw
Comes love, nothing can be done

No one could love you more than I
girl singers of the 1940s
but today I'm in the men's sauna with a poet
from Nepal doing Yoga and the bonhomie
of the men's locker room is what stays with me

And therefore I wish to salute Steve Lawrence
with or without Eydie, and Mel Tormé, Nat Cole,
Joe Williams with the Basie band,
Johnny Hartman, "My One and Only Love," the depth
of that voice matching Coltrane's tenor sax

"Did you know that Trane died on the same day
as Billie Holiday only now it was 1967?"

"I didn't know that but I like it when you call him Trane"

I'd love to get you on a slow boat to China
along with the gong announcing
the end of Sinatra's ode
to Kipling's "On the Road
to Mandalay"

But beautiful

and Bobby Darin could do anything
from "Sundays in New York"
to "Artificial Flowers"

and "Beyond the Sea"
should be compared with Charles Trenet's "La Mer"
as an example of a total translation, both words and music

Meditating how sweet life could be if

and did you know Vic Damone
tried out for the part
of Johnny Fontaine alias Frankie Boy
in *The Godfather* he didn't get it
but the guy who did, Al Martino, sings
Vic Damone's breakout hit at Connie's wedding
"I have but one heart, this love I bring you"
how's that for chutzpah

When I took Julius LaRosa to lunch
he said Sinatra's number one and the next
best is number thirty-seven and the best
singer since is Jack Jones, son of Allan Jones,
the tenor who played opposite Irene Dunne in the 1930s'
Show Boat, and I am thinking of you, Jack,
you bring the giddy 1960s back
wives should always be lovers, too
and even now I can hear you
sing the Chrysler New Yorker commercial
to the tune of "The Talk of the Town"
during the 1975 World Series

A man named Young
wrote "A Hundred Years from Today"
one of the great carpe diem songs
whose premise is youth
is fleeting Victor Young
wrote the music Ned Washington
the lyrics so let's play Jack Teagarden's
Decca recording from 1941
with the moon above,
it's yours and it's mine,
remember, darling, we won't see it shine
a hundred years from today.

I'm listening to Eric Dolphy without understanding a word
there are no words but I know what you mean
on the drive back to Hamilton College
after visiting Archie for the first time
in Goldwin Smith Hall in 1976 I brought my hardcover copy
of *Diversifications* he signed it and took me
to *Epoch* headquarters we took a walk
around the Cornell arts quad he showed me
the one building on campus he liked (was it Barnes Hall?)
because it "has some diversity to go with its unity"
he complained of bad health bad teeth bad skin
well, I said, you look good
well, he said, I fuck a lot

Hey Archie
I thought of dialing your phone number today
257 6181
to see if I can still make you laugh
like the time I called the English department
and asked for you
you weren't there but Margaret took a message
I said Archibald MacLeish called for you
and sure enough
an hour and a half later you returned my call
so today I am phoning you to say
I am going to write a poem you'll like
called "Empty Calories: A Memoir"

On Green Dolphin Street with Miles Davis
While I double-check the record
And yes, according to the official minutes
Churchill ordered a "weak whiskey and soda"
at a crisis meeting in May 1940
I always liked that
and the other accoutrements,
the bowtie the cigar and the waistcoat,
the brandy in the bathtub, naked,
"the Prime Minister of Great Britain
has nothing to hide from the President
of the United States" in the White House.

Come fly with me let's fly let's fly away
On the agenda for the day
Thelonious Monk will play "In Walked Bud"
And Jamie will explain why Monk is the nearest thing
In jazz to abstract expressionism
Then Sonny Rollins will make people grin
When he weaves "doo-dah, doo-dah" into "Misterioso"
And I vote for Nestor Torres ("Cute")
The first Nestor in my life since *The Odyssey*

When I listened to "Ralph's New Blues"
(Modern Jazz Quartet) the epiphany was
the music that remained when the melody
was removed -- even for such as I who
can't think of a better way to say
our love is here to stay than the song.

Archie you must guide me now
be to me what Virgil
was to Dante, what Rousseau
was to Shelley, I made you laugh
today we were talking about *Lolita*
the movie, with Shelley Winters
as the poor mother of the nymphet,
and I said "if Shelley Winters comes,
can spring be far behind?"
Archie, your guide was the wind
Mine is the voice
of Cecile McLorin Salvant, "Nothing
like you has ever been seen before"

I'm trying to catch up it's hard
"Blue Rondo a la Turk" with Al Jarreau
My philosophy about the news is
Ignore the news the way you avert your eyes
From an ugly car crash
Or the stock market on a down day

The greatest nickname
in the history of jazz
is Cannonball Adderley
"The Jive Samba"
Sam Jones with him
In 1963
San Francisco
The Jazz Workshop
Ladies and gentlemen
Here is the saxophonist
You heard on "Kind of Blue"
Brother of cornetist Nat,
"Cannonball" a corruption
Of "cannibal" because
He could eat a horse
Mercy, mercy, mercy

12/7/17

How many times have you heard
the Modern Jazz Quartet
"How High the Moon"
followed by "St. James Infirmary"
and then Armstrong
puts down his trumpet
and Teagarden
puts down his trombone
and they sing "Old Rockin' Chair"

1.

Very dangerous to sing
"I Left My Heart in San Francisco"
If you're not Tony Bennett
But here is Vic Damone
With little cable cars climbing
Halfway to the stars
In front of a hushed audience
Bursting into applause
He had a better voice than Tony
Was he as good a singer
Hard to say depends
Not only on taste but whether
Like Sinatra you value the song
As a dramatic act, a play
In which case you'd have to vote
For Tony, a tenor, while Vic Damone
Is a baritone doesn't that matter?
And they're both still alive as I write

2.

It matters I have to believe that
It does on this sick Friday in December
As I sip the English breakfast tea
With honey that Stacey brewed for me
What a girl what a whirl what a life
I believe that's a quote from the theme
Song of *I Married Joan*, a knock-off
Of *I Love Lucy* with Joan Davis as
Madcap Joan married to Jim Backus,
Who plays a judge
At least he doesn't wear an apron as in
Rebel without a Cause which isn't playing
Today though *Casablanca* is on
How many times have we watched it
And never grow tired of it
What a family, the Epstein brothers
Who wrote the movie, son Leslie
The Boston-based novelist whose son
Theo won the World Series for the Cubs
After having done the same thing in Beantown

3.

"My Kind of Town" is what I'm hearing now
As he swings on stage in front of a whole gang
Of great instrumentalists and there you have
It the definition of swing as he collaborates
With Tony Bennett on a rendition of the song
Each time I leave Chicago is
Grabbing my sleeve there's only one Sinatra
And only one greater song about an American city
You guessed it "New York, New York"
The official song played before the Belmont stakes
I like New York in June I like a Gershwin tune
A Bernstein tune and here comes Billie Holiday
With "A Foggy Day in London Town" and
For a moment or two you feel
The age of miracles hasn't passed.

César Franck's "Violin Sonata in A Major"
(aka "the Franck Sonatra")
We like
I'm glad we settled that
Now if you play Robert Schumann's piano concerto in A minor
I guarantee you'll stop what you're doing and listen
And I find that whenever I'm talking with a serious musicologist,
And the talk turns to the Romantic period,
And he or she says something profound and complicated,
If I say "how about Schumann's piano concerto in A minor?"
My interlocutor will reply as if I've said something intelligent
And make me feel like less of a fraud

Every day is your birthday when
yours is the first voice of the day
in Las Vegas with "Luck Be a Lady"
"Fly Me to the Moon" on Wall Street
"The Best is Yet to Come" in 1966
when one of us was eighteen years old
I see it now

One benefit of writing a book
called *Sinatra's Century*
is I got paid to write a review
of Jack Daniels 100 proof "Sinatra Century"
and drank the bottle
with Stacey in Ithaca
listening to The Voice

You can tell that the guy
who wrote "I'll Be Seeing You"
(in all the old familiar places)
was listening to the *langsam* last movement
of Mahler's third symphony
at the time but in a less
exalted though equally schmaltzy mood

Just as you can be sure that Mahler had
Nietzsche on the brain
in the fourth movement
when the alto asks the deep midnight
to speak and it does it says the world's pain
is deeper than daytime can guess
but pain passes and joy seeks eternity
as do I when I wave my baton

Somewhere some summer a few decades ago,
Mahler's first symphony, "the Titan,"
is playing and melodies familiar from his songs
are turning up with so much *sturm und drang* no wonder
Lenny loved conducting him,
"Frère Jacques" as a funeral march in D minor
dazzling, a double-bass solo no less,
and as for the agitated end, Mahler
storms the heavens "with an apotheosis of D Major"
but only after staring at the abyss and having a good long cry

Before I passed out, Ella Fitzgerald
sang "It's All Right with Me"
Don't you want to forget someone, too
I do
But I am Baudelaire walking among the homeless and I burn
to paint the woman who visits me in my hotel room
and makes a quick exit like an apparition
or something the previous occupant left behind with her nightgown
I burn for her for her black sun and drunk-making moon
To "burn" is to "yearn," a rhyme as natural in the nineteenth century
as "gloomy" and "to me" are in the minds of Johnny Mercer and Leo Robin
and you did say you wanted Harold Arlen to take a bow
with "Blues in the Night" or with Ella singing
"It's only a paper moon" in the context of the great Depression
A critique of "make-believe" that exemplifies what it criticizes
at Honky Tonk U in Penny Lane, PA

Joe Williams has my full attention
speaking of bad luck and trouble
it isn't every day you have the blues
with the Count Basie band backing you up
in the big city where to live is to love is to lose
change achieved one letter at a time
on Malcolm X Boulevard
Ira Gershwin's lyric for "But Not for Me"
Genius
But it's eight o'clock and time for *The Manchurian Candidate*

You ask me to explain Janet Leigh's character
in *The Manchurian Candidate*
and what motivates her to come on to Major Marco
while he is having a cigarette and a nervous
breakdown on the train from DC to NY
perhaps she works for the FBI or CIA
like Eva Marie Saint in *North by Northwest*
but the scenes were left on the cutting-room floor
or maybe she represents the plight
of an attractive woman in pre-feminist days
when the best she can hope for is to be
a nurse or auxiliary to the chain-smoking male hero
on the other hand she wears a pearl necklace
when she gives Sinatra her phone number
Eldorado 5-9970
as if she were a model in a John O'Hara novel
I conclude she needs no further justification for being there
than the fact that she's Janet Leigh

As one who has written on "Hitchcock's America"
I keep waiting for a magazine editor to ask me to write
"Hitchcock's Blondes"
who was the most beautiful of all
Stacey says Grace Kelly and I guess I agree though Ingrid Bergman
as either a spy or a psychoanalyst is to the 1940s
what Grace as a model or a Riviera princess is to the 1950s
and from the point of view of sheer sexuality I don't see how anyone can outdo
Kim Novak in *Vertigo*, for the sophisticated spy you can't beat
Eva Marie Saint in *North by Northwest*,
and for the heroines of *Psycho* and *The Birds*
who could outshine Janet Leigh and Tippi Hedren
who (Tippi) is also well-cast as the kleptomaniac in *Marnie*
who gets to say "You Freud, me Jane?" and "Oh, men!
You say 'no thanks' to one of them and BINGO!
You're a candidate for the funny farm."

I live in Hitchcock's America
What does that mean
It means the ride always ends in an amusement park
and a girl and her uncle can have the same first name
Cary Grant is suave Jimmy Stewart has a broken leg
or a bruised psyche Doris Day's voice fills the house
Even the Jews and the blacks are white
Even the brunettes are blonde
I confess I'm at the end of my rope,
spellbound by the notorious master of suspicion
maybe Janet shouldn't have taken that dough or had that tryst
Joel McCrea tells America that all Europe's lights are out
and Priscilla Lane recites Emma Lazarus's lines
atop the Statue of Liberty

Perfection: Mozart's Piano Concerto no. 20
Delight: Beethoven's Sixth ("the Pastoral")

Why didn't Schubert finish his eighth symphony ("the Unfinished"),
or more exactly why did he write a ninth symphony ("the great")
before finishing the eighth (the greater)?
The classical DJ thinks
maybe Schubert got bored with the piece
not bloody likely
you could counter that he didn't think he could write
a third and fourth movement as good as the first two
so the better part of valor was to quit while he was ahead
it is, of course, possible to argue that it is perfect as is,
whether planned or not,
the immortal melody in the allegro
meeting its match in the clashing sonatinas
of the second movement

Sublime as Schubert's String Quintet in C major
his last and greatest chamber work
now what makes it greater than, say,
the piano quintet known as the Trout
or any of his string quartets?
Maybe because he wrote it with the taste
of death in his mouth in September 1828
and collapsed weeks later weakened by syphilis
and the toxic medications he took for it
dying on November 19
The string quintet has an extra cello
replacing the customary second viola
Maybe that has something to do with it
But when you get to the fourth movement (allegretto)
there's no doubt about it
the music has scored a victory

La chute de reine
is a great French phrase
for the curve at the base of a lady's back
Archie would have approved
after lunch we'd head to Mayer's Smoke Shop
and I'd read *Barron's*
while he ambled over to *Penthouse*
after he found a dime and I, three pennies
on the corner of Tioga and Buffalo where
the old post office used to be
and later that day I wrote
a poem for John Ashbery
let's have it, he said.
okay I said here goes
and John said he liked it
particularly the third line
(the poem was two lines long)

Second shortest day of the year slips into memory with
snow on the branches of tall maples giving them
the look of birches, the ground covered
with Irving Berlin's white dream, virginal
except for the footsteps between me and the mailbox
the sky divided between the blue clouds
and the gray like the uniforms in a bowl game
on television with the sound turned off so I can
listen to Billie Holiday sing "Nice Work if You Can Get It"
or maybe to something rougher like Mingus's "Tonight at Noon'"
where "all hell's about to break out," an idiom Ashbery favored
I'd like to write an homage to JA that begins "I had tried
every pillow out there and none of them worked" but first
the orange ball dips out of sight

Arrived in Ithaca to the smell of gas
NYSEG sent a nice lady in jeans
who swore like a seaman but
fixed the leak, left, smiled, refused a tip,
and Stacey handled the other crises
tomorrow I'll treat myself to a haircut and shave
with Joe the barber who was named after Joe DiMaggio
and keeps in shape by boxing
then to the stamp and coin store downtown but today
I play "Reflections" by Thelonious Monk
and Sinatra "At Sundown" in *The Joker is Wild*
there's still light enough in the white strips
across the light gray sky
which darkens as the day goes by
very slowly and the trees grow taller
without their leaves and the wind
in the evergreens is benign.
I swear, you live here
and you become a nature poet.

Vladimir Horowitz is playing Sousa's "Stars and Stripes Forever"
and the piano sounds like all the instruments in a marching band
without ever ceasing to be a piano, most majestic of instruments,
and didn't Balanchine choreograph a ballet to the same music
a triumph of legs hot dogs and the fourth of July
but the nice thing about turning your room into a radio
is that you can then turn around and play Beethoven's Fifth and relish
the moment when the third movement turns into the fourth

The day begins with a cup of Peggy Lee and black coffee,
Chick Corea, "Sweet and Lovely," and Art Blakey, "Blues March,"
If you're a great actor and you can't make hay playing Churchill
in May 1940, buddy, you're in the wrong line of work
so tonight it's up to you, Gary Oldman,
and I'm feeling a lift because
the light moving westward is joyous
and Oscar Peterson goes from "Swinging on a Star"
to "How High the Moon"
and then I listen to "Giant Steps"
John Coltrane on tenor sax
three keys, a major third, an augmented triad,
as if for the first time

"One O'Clock Jump" with Count Basie now
that'll grab your attention and when it's
over you change stations and you get
the saxophone and piano solos in
Charlie Parker "Out of Nowhere" but
there are days you have to mute the sound
and listen to the dialogue in *The Godfather*
my theory is that lines spoken to Tom Hagen
have a special importance throughout
I don't like violence, Tom. I'm a businessman.
Blood is a big expense. I don't feel I have
to wipe everybody out, Tom. Just my enemies.
Tom, this is business and this man
is taking it very, very personal.
Can you get me off the hook, Tom,
for old time's sake?

On Marlene Dietrich's 116th birthday
she wears a top hat for me and sings with a lovely lisp
she knows what she wants, *einen Mann einen richtigen Mann*
Christmas music on most stations but
Wynton Marsalis on mine
"Can't get started with you"
one of Ira's finest lyrics
with music by Vladimir Dukelsky
alias Vernon Duke
on the jazz station
and then comes Chet Baker, owner of the youngest voice
of all time, an old man singing "Imagination,"
a young man's song, not much of a lyric but a lovely tune

.

"Denmark's a prison."
Substitute "marriage."
This was when one was twenty-six or twenty-eight
and one yearned to go to prison
which was located in Copenhagen
not far from the Tivoli Gardens
which you must visit if you go to Copenhagen.
One even committed crimes solely
for the purpose of getting caught
and sentenced to prison there.
The time in solitary
would be the time it took to write a book
as crazy as *Mein Kampf*.
The time would go as slowly
as time on a hot September afternoon
when one has vowed to fast until sundown.

You stepped out of a cloud
Thanks to Johnny Hartman
Then a Churchill speech "Now we are masters of our fate"
Mussolini even then a laugh-line
"What kind of a people do they think we are?
"Don't they realize we will never cease?"
I drive to Wegman's stock up on oranges and limes then
A bottle of Cherry Heering at Northside to try a Singapore Sling
On the theory that everyone needs to try a Singapore Sling at least once
Twice if you add Contratto Bitter and Key West lime juice

March on, march on, but first let's dance
a ballet blanc with Chopin's *Les Sylphides*
on a nuit blanche the ballerina in white
the shape of a bell the dress down to her calves
You do feel like cheering but tell me what
does this have to do with Stravinsky's
Soldier's Tale-Suite, which follows,
sounding Russian to my ears as Mozart's
piano concerto no. 27 in B flat sounds Viennese
now why is that I don't know but that's what
I am thinking when the strings take over
the woodwinds interrupt
like birds on spring mornings and the mood
is lively with a fantastic script
now if I could only put it into words

I can't wait for five o'clock
to listen to Duke Elington, "Cocktails for Two"
and maybe it makes a difference maybe not
but I am going to use the high priced vermouth
with the small-batch gin and a pearl onion
stir with mucho jalo and serve with one ice cube
now I'm in the mood for "Broadway" with
Mel Tormé where the joy of living holds sway
and a great underrated song like "Memories of You"
for Sinatra in 1957 or for Art Tatum on solo piano
or for Benjamin David Goodman on clarinet
in conversation with Fletcher Henderson at the piano
and Lionel Hampton on the vibraphone
now I want to hear it sung so Rosemary Clooney
follows Benny's clarinet in 1956

Happy new year as I was saying Artie Shaw
disbands his troupe goes to Mexico
comes back with "Frenesi" I play that
and follow with "Amapola," the background music
as heartsore Noodles pursues Deborah
in *Once Upon a Time in America*, and "Perfidia,"
the background music in the scene
where the petty Yugoslav bureaucrat gets blackmailed
for state secrets in *The Mask of Dimitrios* with Zachary
Scott as Dimitrios, perfect for the part, and
the fourth of my one-word foreign titles is "Volare"
with Dean Martin sliding into an evening in Roma,
always lifts my spirits, and then
Sinatra (1954), Lee Wylie (1934), June Hutton (1961),
Maxine Sullivan when she was seventy-five
and Sarah Vaughan take turns
singing from beyond the boundary
 "A Hundred Years from Today"

Brahms expected his close friends to leap to their feet
and say bravo but their misgivings woke his own
and there were only three weeks to go, so he had no choice
but to forge ahead with his fourth
in E minor, opus 98, a restless allegro
beginning with two notes in a falling third.
"For the whole of that movement I felt as if
I was getting beaten up by two very intelligent people."
Brief melancholy, the winds are lovely, the guide says
"tragic pathos" and maybe Jan Swofford is right who says
minor-key dramas usually move "from darkness to light
and fatality to triumph by turning to the major mode by
the end, but here the culmination is resolutely minor."
Still, I'm with the guy who hears the ring of defiance.

"Step Lightly" with Bobby Hutcherson (vibes)
fourteen minutes nineteen seconds
then the 1963 recording of the same song
by Blue Mitchell (trumpet) with Joe Henderson
and Herbie Hancock. You don't have to choose:
that's the beauty of it. I learned this one evening
when we had guests and I put on a disc consisting
entirely of versions of "All of Me": Sinatra,
Billie Holiday, Ruth Etting, Mildred Bailey,
Harry James, Count Basie, Benny Goodman,
Louis Armstrong, Teddy Wilson, Dinah Washington,
others too, and the volume was low
and no one was listening
until a break in the conversation and Nic Christopher
who said "hey, this is great music" won the prize

Dorisb4day is a great screen name because
of Oscar Levant's witticism (he knew Doris Day
"before she was a virgin") but mostly because
of the voice of Doris at break of day or when
driving on Rte. 17 and listening to her sing
"Sentimental Journey" with Les Brown ("and
his band of renown") and "Dream a Little Dream
of Me" or "Someone Like You," "A Hundred Years
from Today," or "Love Me or Leave Me,"
the face cherubic, the flip side of Sinatra's
brooding in *Young at Heart*, blonde
and relentlessly upbeat, but there is sex in that voice

Mozart's twenty-fifth symphony, written when
he was seventeen, known as "the little G-minor
symphony" to distinguish it from his fortieth
symphony, "the great G-minor symphony"
and the height of Western Civilization,
is moving the traffic nicely on route 13
where yesterday's snow has been swept
but you get to see it on the trees and the hills

It looks like Tennessee is rallying back
from 21 -3 at halftime they've scored twice
they've got the momentum
like the whole technology sector of the market
"Skylark" is even better than "Stardust"
we agree on that and on liking certain euphemisms
such as "whoopee," "it," and "nothing" as
Hamlet uses the word when lying
in Ophelia's lap
who's we? Ray Eberle, Dinah Shore, Helen Forrest
and Bing Crosby, all of whom sang "Skylark" in 1942
and Ella and Louis ("Let's Do It")
and Sinatra in 1956 ("Makin' Whoopee")

Evening summer breeze warbling of a meadowlark
My mother was born today if I lighted a candle for her last evening
My new favorite word is "if"
"If" is the foundation of all fantasy and much poetry
which is an homage to the subjunctive mood
as Robert Musil wrote
And didn't Woody Allen quote
"What Is This Thing Called Love?"
Sinatra seems intent on proving he could hold a note longer
than you'd have thought possible in "April in Paris" ("reprise")
today he is touring the cities the states
beginning with Vermont, then Paris, London by night, Brazil,
Stacey calls from the kitchen "Jon Hamm is on WNYC"
Let Dorothy Fields be your teacher and don't blame me
or Sidney Bechet with "Muskrat Ramble" which
Country Joe and the Fish turned into an antiwar song

There are two things all investors need to know
Don't sell your winners
And
It's always a good time to take some money off the table
Now how you implement these contradictory adages is anyone's guess
But this I know
Jazz is the music of the stock market
As it zigs and zags, from "Dearly Beloved" (Sonny Rollins),
To "September Song" (Gary Burton),
 "Blue Rondo a la Turk (Chris Brubeck),
"Sermonette" (Lambert, Hendricks, and Ross) and
"Honeysuckle Rose" (Ella Fitzgerald)
All on my playlist for today
A Facebook friend asks if I have one piece of advice and only one
To give a young writer, what would it be?
And I say
"Play Count Basie, 'April in Paris,' and write"

Lew Saul reads my two-line poem for him
(See December 18) and adds
"*Le Sacre du Printemps* for air-conducting
on a perfect breezy spring day in Paris
47 years ago" in my room,
where he also played recordings of
Tchaikovsky's Fifth, Beethoven's Grosse Fugue,
and Frank Zappa at the Fillmore East, 1971.
Bravo, Lew. And here's a piece by
Eduard Toldra, "Nocturno," which I don't know,
do you? It seems to be a prelude
to Tchaikovsky's Piano Trio in A minor
which itself seems to be a prelude
in the sense Wordsworth gave the word.

Thanks to Nat King Cole
there's an orange colored sky
and the Dow is now
in positive territory
erasing earlier losses
The two most boring words
in the language are
"Russia investigation"
Rod Stewart trying to sing Gershwin
is even sadder than Sinatra wasting
his voice on "Winchester Cathedral"
and if Ravel wrote
a pavanne for the princess
of Monaco he wasn't thinking
of Grace Kelly
but I can

On the bad news station
they're doing interactive
multiple choice questions
such as: "The difference
between fifty and one
hundred dollars is (1) a lot,
(2) an insignificant sum,
(3) fifty per-cent, or
(4) the difference between
fifty and one hundred
dollars." Then the host
introduces a guest
who will, on the basis
of your answer, tell you
how you will vote in
the next election.

Someday my prince will come
and Miles Davis is his name
the more I see you the more I hear
Johnny Hartman in the next apartment
I sat on a bar stool next to Stephanie Paterik
we sang "Good Morning" and the girl
one stool over joined in and we agreed
there are three reasons to watch
There's No Business Like Show Business
and those three reasons are
the three songs Marilyn sings
not to mention how she seduces the lyrics
of "Bye-Bye Baby" in *Gentlemen Prefer Blondes*
and the pathos she finds in Gus Kahn's lyric
for "I'm Through with Love" in *Some Like it Hot*

Upstairs Stacey is listening to Beethoven's first piano concerto
Downstairs the Philadelphia Orchestra is doing Mahler's fifth symphony
and wait until tonight you will hear
the march from *Aida* in Les Brown's "Swingin' at the Met"
and "Tangerine" (as a Bob Eberly ballad, then
Helen O'Connell, fast-paced and satirical)
and Hoagy Carmichael's "Rockin' Chair" he gets it,
he gets it. When the time comes to make a change,
"rhythm is our business," Jimmie Lunceford declares,
and in "Scenes in the City" (Branford Marsalis) it ain't
like women in a magazine, "Frim Fram Sauce,"
(he gets it), and "Odds Against Tomorrow"

I began thinking
that listing the titles
would be poetry
enough and now it is
thirty degrees and rising
in Ithaca with the dazzle
of sunlight like
diamond spangles
in the snow, the sky
blue and cumulus
clouds drift slowly south

Tonight son Joe and I
will watch *The Seven Samurai*
until then I must work
on my foreword with
Bill Evans, "Round
Midnight," backing me up
while the sun
shines right through
the shades so I can't even see
the type on the screen

on the forties station
Frances Langford,
"Serenade in Blue,"
with its amazing
mood-shifting bridge
"but you remained in my heart"

The agenda for today
is Nureyev dancing to
Nat Cole singing
"Nature Boy" and I,
happy to be alive,
sad to bring this
poem to an end,
propose a toast to Archie

and what did we
accomplish along the way
did we communicate
did we say anything new
or something old in a new way
or something borrowed
something blue the color
of the sky today despite the
zero-at-the-bone temperature
the music was great
from Ithaca to New York City
with you beside me.